cocktails

cocktails

James Butler and Vicki Liley

PERIPLUS

contents

Introduction **6**

Glassware **8**

Measurements **9**

Equipment **10**

Mixing techniques **12**

Ingredients **14**

Garnishes and decorations **16**

Food ideas **20**

Classic cocktails **24**

Champagne cocktails **42**

Martinis **48**

Blended cocktails **58**

Crushed cocktails **74**

Built cocktails **82**

Shaken and strained cocktails **94**

Nonalcoholic cocktails **102**

Hot drinks **106**

Glossary **108**

Index **110**

The cocktail was born in the United States in the nineteenth century. Exactly who and where remains controversial, but there's no denying that the United States has been almost single-handedly responsible for the drink's popularity and growth.

These days, there are more cocktails than you can count. Virtually any alcoholic liquid and flavoring can be combined, and new cocktails are being invented all the time. Most are based on spirits and served chilled or with ice. They can be as simple as a classic martini or as complex as a margarita, where citrus juice and tequila are sipped from a glass rimmed with salt.

The way you mix a cocktail depends on its ingredients, but it's an art easily mastered. Liquids of similar densities can be stirred. Limpid, transparent ingredients call for gentle stirring, as too much agitation can cause the cocktail to turn cloudy. Vigorous agitation is called for, however,

introduction

when mixing liquids of different densities: spirits and syrups or liqueurs, as in a margarita.

You'll find that a genuine cocktail shaker will come in handy, as it allows you to chill and blend ingredients simultaneously. Ice is added to the shaker, but is prevented by a strainer from entering the glass.

Another useful item is a blender, for preparing cocktails that include solid ingredients. Fruit, for example, can be reduced to a purée, and ice cubes cracked into smaller pieces give a daiquiri its pleasantly granular texture. Some cocktails containing solid ingredients rely for their success on the aromatic flavors of oils being released into the glass. If you're preparing a caipirinha, you'll need to use a muddler (see page 11) or the back of a spoon to crush the cut fruit and extract that unmistakable fresh citrus taste. Mint juleps call for mint leaves and sugar to be ground together to enhance the drink's citrus overtones.

And let's not forget the ice. It's not there simply to cool the drink. Whole ice cubes melt slowly and are best when you want maximum coldness with minimum dilution. Crushed ice introduces its own texture but also melts quickly enough to dilute a strong drink. Whichever kind of ice you use, remember that cubes made with bottled water frozen shortly before using will taste a whole lot better than that chlorinated liquid you get from a tap. Don't ruin good liquor with bad water.

Above all, don't forget that cocktails are meant to be fun. It doesn't matter whether they're classic and sophisticated or modern and innovative. They can be served at an intimate dinner party—before, during or after—or just to unwind after a hard day.

But wherever cocktails are served, they introduce a touch of glamour that you just don't get with other drinks.

glassware

Everyone agrees a drink tastes much better when served in a beautiful glass and a cocktail seems to have more importance when it is served in a special glass.

The Champagne flute:

8–14 fl oz (250–430 ml)

Elegant and long stemmed, with a narrow rim, the Champagne flute is artfully designed to conserve the natural bubbles in Champagne.

The martini and cocktail glass:

6–8 fl oz (180–250 ml)

The martini glass has an open face, a thin stem and a V-shaped bowl. The cocktail glass is similar, but has a slightly rounded bowl. It is not essential to have both glasses.

The highball or Collins glass:

8–10 fl oz (250–310 ml)

The highball, or Collins, glass can vary greatly in style and size, but is always tall and slim, designed to keep a long drink cold.

The old-fashioned or rocks glass:

6–10 fl oz (180–310 ml)

The old-fashioned, or rocks, glass is short and straight sided. It has a heavy base and is comfortable to hold. Drinks served in these glasses are generally meant to be enjoyed slowly.

Note on measurements

Please note that all alcohol measurements in this book are given in fl oz and ml.
1–1½ fl oz (30–45 ml) is approximately equivalent to one jigger.
½ fl oz (15 ml) is equivalent to one US/UK tablespoon. ⅔ fl oz (20 ml) is equivalent to one Australian tablespoon.
All recipes serve 1.

equipment

Shaker:

There are two types: the most common, available in department stores, is the stainless-steel cocktail shaker. This usually consists of three parts: a small lid, the strainer, and the receptacle. Before shaking a drink, always make sure that the shaker is assembled correctly. The other type of shaker is called a Boston shaker; it is half stainless steel, half glass.

Having the correct bar equipment for constructing cocktails will make the experience more fun and enjoyable.

Bar spoon:

A bar spoon is a long, flat-headed spoon with a twisted shaft, used for stirring drinks in a mixing glass, pouring layered drinks, and muddling or crushing.

Muddler:

A muddler is a wooden pestle used for mixing or crushing ingredients such as sugar cubes, limes and mint. If you don't have one, use a mortar and pestle, then transfer the ingredients to a glass.

Jigger:

A double-headed jigger is best. It holds liquid measures of 1 fl oz (30 ml) and 1½ fl oz (45 ml).

Strainer:

A strainer is used to pour shaken drinks through into the glass. The Hawthorn strainer (pictured) has a spring coiled around its head. The spring fits neatly inside a mixing glass to hold the strainer in place.

Other equipment

Other useful equipment for your cocktail bar includes measuring spoons and cups, a citrus juicer, an ice bucket and ice tongs, and a blender.

mixing techniques

Muddling:

The process of pressing and pounding a wooden pestle into fruit, sugar and/or herbs in the base of a heavy old-fashioned or rocks glass. Muddling allows flavors to be released gently.

Shaking:

Shaking cocktails can be fun for you and your guests. Fill a shaker with ice cubes before adding your favorite cocktail ingredients. Shake up and down for about 10 seconds, a little longer for cocktails with egg white and/or cream bases. Always make sure you hold the lid while shaking. Remove the lid and strain the contents into the desired glass.

Stirring:

This is the best method when you require clarity of the spirits. Martinis, for example, should always be stirred. Use an ice-filled glass, and stir carefully with a bar spoon. Another method is to gently swirl the spirits in an ice-filled cocktail shaker, then strain them into a chilled glass. With both methods, be careful not to chip the ice, thus diluting the drink.

Blending:

Ice and the cocktail ingredients are combined in a blender and blended until smooth.

Building:

This is the simplest method of making cocktails. The measured cocktail ingredients are added to an ice-filled glass and given, if needed, a quick stir.

ingredients

Flavored spirits:

Any spirit can be flavored with a variety of fruits, herbs and spices, from chili to citrus. Add your chosen flavoring to your favorite spirit, seal and let stand in a cool, dark place for at least 1 month.

Fruit purée:

Put a small amount of the desired fruit in a food processor or blender and add 1 tablespoon sugar syrup. Blend until smooth. Use as required in fruit cocktails.

Sugar syrup:

In a small saucepan, combine 1 cup (8 oz/250 g) sugar and 1 cup (8 fl oz/250 ml) water. Bring to a boil over medium heat, stirring until sugar dissolves. Remove from heat and let cool. Pour into a bottle, seal and store in the refrigerator.

Syrups:

These commercial syrups add complexity and flavor to a drink. Usually nonalcoholic or quite low in alcohol (less than 3 percent), they come in many flavors, including cherry, strawberry, raspberry, coconut, pineapple and ginger.

garnishes and decorations

For some people it's not a real cocktail unless there's a garnish on the side of the glass. Garnishes can be as simple as a citrus twist or a single olive on a toothpick, or you may want to create a party atmosphere and decorate your cocktails with colorful, fun decorations.

Cucumber shavings make impressive garnishes for savory-based drinks. Using a vegetable peeler, shave thin lengthwise slices from a cucumber. Twist in a glass before filling with ice and the cocktail ingredients.

Plastic mermaids and the like are fun, colorful and make great conversation starters at parties.

Flavored ices: Fill ice cube trays with fruit juice and add to your favorite cocktails.

Kitschy drink stirrers make simple garnishes for cocktails in old-fashioned and highball glasses.

Fresh flowers and fruit leaves make simple garnishes for fruit- and cream-based cocktails.

Paper parasols are available in a wide variety of colors and patterns. Popular in the 1970s, these cute little icons are enjoying a return to popularity in many cocktail bars.

Garnished rims: Rub a cut lime or lemon along the rim of the glass and then upend into a saucer filled with either sea salt, white pepper or sugar. Sugar can be colored by adding a drop or two of food coloring and mixing thoroughly.

Fresh berries make tasteful, simple and edible garnishes. Citrus twists, wedges and slices also make good garnishes for most cocktails, as do fresh pineapple leaves, maraschino cherries and mint sprigs.

food ideas

Try these quick and easy nibbles with your cocktails!

Wrap prosciutto around small chunks of melon.

Team cubes of watermelon and feta cheese. Sprinkle with fresh thyme leaves and a drizzle of virgin olive oil.

Serve fresh oysters in their shell with a squeeze of fresh lime juice.

Deep-fry shavings (use a vegetable peeler) of fresh parsnip until golden and crisp, then sprinkle with sea salt.

Marinate black and green olives in a blend of olive oil, chopped chili and herbs.

Fry your favorite nut selection in vegetable oil until golden. Toss in a mixture of sea salt and cayenne pepper.

Serve crunchy bread sticks with soda-based drinks.

Top crostini with a finely chopped mix of tomato, red onion, cilantro (fresh coriander), balsamic vinegar, salt and pepper.

classic cocktails

"Classic: a work of enduring excellence."
—*Webster's Tenth New Collegiate Dictionary*

Classic cocktails are an exclusive club—one with just a few distinguished members but the largest fan club since Elvis. And they're the best way to test a new bar or mixologist. Ask for a classic you know and love, then keep score. Do they use a good, dark rum in the mai tai? Is the Bellini made with fresh peaches? Is the sea breeze bitter, yet thirst-quenching? This is the kind of exam the bar staff will need to pass to get into Cocktail College!

It really shouldn't be too difficult. The following classics have been around for years, most of them for decades, and they've stood the tests of time, fashion and fad. Like a good cigar, they're straightforward and have a certain dignity about them. Content to wait in the wings while more exotic, upstart creations have their fifteen minutes of fame, the classics are today more popular than ever.

Like timeless movies or tunes, classic cocktails are conversation starters, historical icons, and definitions of good taste that bring with them the memories of special times and places. And you know what they say about the benefits of a classical education, so put your head down and study a few of these before you send out your next invitations, whether the gathering is sophisticated or casual. There's a lot to be said for the keep-it-simple formula when it comes to party drinks, and these smooth-talkers know exactly how to say "welcome."

classic cocktails

Long Island iced tea

ice cubes
1 fl oz (30 ml) vodka
1 fl oz (30 ml) gin
1 fl oz (30 ml) light rum
1 fl oz (30 ml) tequila
1 fl oz (30 ml) lemon juice
Coca-Cola, chilled

Fill a highball glass with ice cubes. Add vodka, gin, rum, tequila and lemon juice. Top with Coca-Cola and stir.

Singapore sling

ice cubes
1 fl oz (30 ml) gin
1 fl oz (30 ml) lemon juice
dash of Cointreau
dash of Bénédictine
dash of pineapple juice
dash of Cherry Heering liqueur
Singapore orchid for garnish

Fill a highball glass with ice cubes. Add gin, lemon juice, Cointreau, Bénédictine and pineapple juice, and stir. Pour Cherry Heering into the center of the drink. Garnish with Singapore orchid.

Above: Singapore sling
Left: Long Island iced tea

classic cocktails

Manhattan

(Perfect)

3 fl oz (90 ml)
Canadian whiskey
½ fl oz (15 ml) Dry vermouth
½ fl oz (15 ml)
Sweet Vermouth
dash of angostura bitters
stemmed cherry or
lemon twist for garnish

Pour ingredients into mixing glass. Sitr and strain into a small chilled martini glass. Garnish with a stemmed cherry.

(Dry)
As above but without sweet vermouth. Garnish with a lemon twist.

(Sweet)
As above but without dry vermouth. Garnish with a stemmed cherry.

James Bond

1 sugar cube
angostura bitters
for soaking
1 fl oz (30 ml) vodka
Champagne, chilled

Soak sugar cube with angostura bitters. Put sugar cube in a Champagne saucer or flute. Pour vodka over sugar and top with Champagne.

Above: James Bond

Moscow mule

ice cubes
2 lime wedges
2 fl oz (60 ml) vodka
½ fl oz (15 ml) lime juice
ginger beer, chilled
fresh pineapple leaves
for garnish

Fill a highball glass with ice cubes and add lime wedges. Add vodka and lime juice. Top with ginger beer and stir. Garnish with pineapple leaves.

Bellini

1 peach wedge
½ fresh ripe peach, peeled and pitted
½ fl oz (15 ml) peach liqueur
Champagne, chilled

Put peach wedge in a Champagne flute. Put peach half in a blender. Purée and pour into glass. Add peach liqueur and top with Champagne. Stir gently.

classic cocktails

Kir royale

¼ fl oz (7½ ml) crème de cassis
Champagne, chilled

Pour crème de cassis into a Champagne flute. Top with chilled Champagne.

Gimlet

ice cubes
2 fl oz (60 ml) Gin
lime cordial or lime juice
lime twist for garnish

In a mixing glass, combine ingredients with ice, stir and strain into a chilled martini glass. Garnish with a lime twist.

Above: Kir royale

classic cocktails

Pina Colada

ice cubes
1½ fl oz (45 ml) rum
2 fl oz (60 ml) pineapple juice
¼ cup (2 fl oz/60 ml) cream of coconut
2 pineapple leaves or 1 sprig of mint for garnish

Combine all ingredients in a shaker and mix. Serve over ice, or blend with crushed ice. Garnish with 2 pineapple leaves or a sprig of mint.

Caipirinha

1 lime, cut into eighths
3 brown sugar cubes
ice cubes
2 fl oz (60 ml) cachaça

Put lime and sugar cubes into an old-fashioned glass. Muddle until juice is extracted and sugar is crushed. Fill glass with ice cubes and top with cachaça. Mix well.

Above: Caipirinha

Margarita

ice cubes
2 fl oz (60 ml) tequila
1 fl oz (30 ml) Cointreau
1 fl oz (30 ml) lemon juice
1 fl oz (30 ml) lime juice
dash of lightly beaten egg white
coarse salt for garnish

Fill a cocktail shaker with ice cubes. Add tequila, Cointreau, lemon juice, lime juice and egg white. Shake and strain into a salt-rimmed martini glass.

classic cocktails

Grasshopper

ice cubes
1 fl oz (30 ml) green crème de menthe
1 fl oz (30 ml) white crème de cacao
2 tablespoons heavy (double) cream
sugar for garnish

Fill a cocktail shaker with ice cubes. Add crème de menthe, crème de cacao and cream. Shake and strain into a sugar-rimmed martini glass.

Sea breeze

ice cubes
2 lime wedges
2 fl oz (60 ml) vodka
cranberry juice, chilled
grapefruit juice, chilled
1 lime slice for garnish

Fill a highball or Collins glass with ice cubes and squeeze lime wedges over ice. Pour in vodka. Fill glass three-fourths full with cranberry juice, top with grapefruit juice, and stir. Garnish with lime slice.

Above: Grasshopper
Left: Sea breeze

classic cocktails

Mint julep

5–6 fresh mint leaves
2 sugar cubes
ice cubes
3 fl oz (90 ml) bourbon

Muddle mint and sugar together in an old-fashioned glass until juice is extracted and sugar is crushed. Fill glass with ice. Pour bourbon over ice and stir.

Tom Collins

ice cubes
1 fl oz (30 ml) lemon juice
1 fl oz (30 ml) gin
dash of sugar syrup
soda water, chilled
1 lemon slice for garnish

Fill a highball glass with ice. Add lemon juice, gin and sugar syrup. Top with soda water and stir. Garnish with lemon slice.

Cosmopolitan

ice cubes
2 fl oz (60 ml)
Absolut Citron vodka
1 fl oz (30 ml) Cointreau
1 fl oz (30 ml) lime juice
1 fl oz (30 ml) cranberry juice
dash of lightly beaten
egg white
fresh pineapple leaves
for garnish

Fill a cocktail shaker with ice cubes. Add vodka, Cointreau, lime juice, cranberry juice and egg white. Shake and strain into a large martini glass. Garnish with pineapple leaves.

Daiquiri

ice cubes
2 fl oz (60 ml)
Bacardi white rum
2 fl oz (60 ml) lime juice
dash of sugar syrup
1 lime wedge for garnish

Fill a cocktail shaker with ice. Add rum, lime juice and sugar syrup. Shake and strain into a chilled cocktail or large martini glass. Garnish with lime wedge.

classic cocktails

Mojito

5 fresh mint leaves
2 sugar cubes
2 lime wedges
ice cubes
2 fl oz (60 ml)
Bacardi white rum
soda water, chilled

Put mint leaves and sugar cubes in an old-fashioned glass. Muddle until sugar is crushed. Add lime wedges. Muddle again until juice is extracted. Fill glass with ice. Pour rum over ice, top with soda water, and stir.

Bloody Mary

ice cubes
2 fl oz (60 ml) vodka
½ fl oz (15 ml) lemon juice
6 fl oz (180 ml) tomato juice
dash of Tabasco sauce
2 dashes Worcestershire sauce
1 teaspoon horseradish sauce
ground white pepper, celery stick, and pinch of ground black pepper for garnish

Half fill a cocktail shaker with ice cubes. Add vodka, lemon juice, tomato juice and sauces. Shake and strain into a glass with a white pepper rim. Garnish with a celery stick and black pepper.

Above: Mojito

classic cocktails

Rob Roy

ice cubes
1½ fl oz (45 ml) scotch
¾ fl oz (23 ml) sweet vermouth
lemon twist for garnish

In a mixing glass, combine ingredients with ice, stir and strain into a chilled martini glass. If desired, garnish with a lemon twist.

Brandy Alexander

ice cubes
2 fl oz (60 ml) brandy
½ fl oz (15 ml) crème de cacao
1 tablespoon half-and-half cream (half milk, half cream)
ground nutmeg for dusting

Fill a cocktail shaker with ice. Add brandy, crème de cacao and cream. Shake and pour into a cocktail glass. Dust with nutmeg.

Above: Brandy Alexander

Mai tai

1 long strip orange zest
ice cubes
1½ fl oz (45 ml) light rum
⅓ fl oz (10 ml) curaçao
⅓ fl oz (10 ml) lime juice
½ fl oz (15 ml) pineapple juice
dash of angostura bitters
2 dashes orgeat syrup
fresh mint leaves and
1 orange wedge for garnish

Wind zest into a highball glass. Fill glass and a cocktail shaker with ice. Add rum, curaçao, juices, bitters and orgeat syrup to shaker. Shake and strain into ice-filled glass. Garnish with mint leaves and orange wedge.

champagne cocktails

"Champagne and orange juice is a great drink. The orange improves the Champagne. The Champagne definitely improves the orange."
—*Prince Philip, Duke of Edinburgh*

Why is it that Champagne (with or without the uppercase "C" reserved for the "real McCoy" from the Champagne region of northeast France) always makes you feel happy, even bringing out a sense of humor in the normally dour duke? Served in a cocktail at a party or as a pre-dinner drink, this nose-tingling fizz imparts a fabulous sense of fun and enjoyment, and an expectation of good times ahead.

There's the school of thought that claims Champagne is best enjoyed chilled and on its own. But a fine-tasting Champagne can actually be improved by mixing it with ingredients that enhance its taste. The results can be absolutely stunning!

Well-known classic Champagne cocktails, such as James Bond, Bellini and kir royale (see pages 28, 30 and 31), happily marry chilled Champagne with just one other simple flavoring.

If you can't afford French Champagne, substitute a good sparkling wine from California. These New World "champagnes" are made from the same grapes (chardonnay, pinot noir or pinot blanc) as their French cousins, frequently by U.S. subsidiaries of the French parent. There are also endless varieties of German sekt or Italian spumante that work just as well.

What are the rules for Champagne cocktail success? (1) Keep it simple; (2) Always use chilled Champagne; (3) Always add the Champagne to the cocktail last (that way you'll keep the bubbles bubbling); (4) Don't expect the taste of a cheap Champagne to improve when used in a cocktail.

champagne cocktails

French 75

ice cubes
½ fl oz (15 ml) gin
½ fl oz (15 ml) lemon juice
dash of sugar syrup
Champagne, chilled

Fill a highball glass with ice. Add gin, lemon juice and sugar syrup. Top with Champagne and stir.

Peach bubbles

ice cubes
⅓ fl oz (10 ml) peach schnapps
dash of peach nectar
ruby red grapefruit juice
Champagne, chilled

Fill a highball glass with ice. Pour schnapps and peach nectar over ice. Half fill glass with grapefruit juice. Top with Champagne. If desired, garnish with a wedge of ruby red grapefruit.

*Above: Peach bubbles (front)
and French 75 (back)*

Alasia

2 teaspoons raspberry purée
½ fl oz (15 ml) crème de framboise
Champagne, chilled
3 fresh raspberries for garnish

Pour raspberry purée and crème de framboise into a Champagne flute. Top with Champagne. Garnish with raspberries.

One-five-one

1 sugar cube
dash of sour cherry syrup
1 fl oz (30 ml)
Bacardi 151 rum
Champagne, chilled

Put sugar cube in a Champagne flute and pour cherry syrup over. Add rum and top with Champagne.

champagne cocktails

Croatian cherry

½ fl oz (15 ml)
sour cherry syrup
½ fl oz (15 ml) sloe gin
Champagne, chilled
cherries for garnish

Pour syrup and sloe gin into
a Champagne flute. Top
with Champagne. If desired,
garnish with cherries.

Adam's apple

1 apple slice or small
apple wedge
⅓ fl oz (10 ml) Calvados
Champagne, chilled

Put apple slice or wedge in
a Champagne flute. Add
Calvados and top with
Champagne.

Left: Croatian cherry (front),
Adam's apple (middle),
One-five-one (back)

martinis

> "The three-martini lunch is the epitome of American efficiency. Where else can you get an earful, a bellyful, and a snootful at the same time?"
> —*Gerald R. Ford*

The origins of the martini are as shrouded in mystery as the origins of the cocktail itself. Some say it first appeared in New York, others favor San Francisco. More likely is that it was named for the Martini & Rossi company, makers of the famous vermouth.

Regardless of its origins, there's no doubting that the classic gin and vermouth martini has spawned more variations than just about any other drink on the planet. Thanks to the martini's great fertility, you may now never have the same martini twice, but, in the proper hands, you can have a superb martini every time. In this book, we've gone for vodka as the "parent" element for our martinis. The popularity of vodka in recent times has seen it overtake gin as the preferred base, and it still imparts the classic lightness and dryness that epitomize the martini.

Whether you're keeping an eye on the bartender or mixing them at home, make sure your martini is served in a chilled martini or cocktail glass. It's even a good idea to keep a few glasses in the freezer for when those unexpected guests drop in. Remember to always consume this tipple immediately, while it's still icy cold—a quick drink also gives you a legitimate excuse for a second round!

martinis

Killer martini

ice cubes
3 fl oz (90 ml) vodka
1 pimiento-stuffed
green olive and
1 teaspoon blue cheese
for garnish

Half fill a cocktail shaker with ice and add vodka. Stir and strain into a chilled martini glass. Remove pimiento from olive and fill center with blue cheese. Garnish martini with stuffed olive.

Scud martini

ice cubes
3 fl oz (90 ml)
chili-infused vodka
1 small fresh red chili and
1 green olive for garnish

Half fill a cocktail shaker with ice. Add vodka. Stir and strain into a chilled martini glass. Garnish with chili and olive.

Above: Scud martini
Right: Killer martini

martinis

Crown martini

ice cubes
⅓ fl oz (10 ml) Chambord
1 fl oz (30 ml) vodka
½ fl oz (15 ml) lemon juice
½ fl oz (15 ml) grapefruit juice

Half fill a cocktail shaker with ice. Add Chambord, vodka and juices. Stir and strain into a chilled martini glass.

Rose water and cinnamon martini

ice cubes
3 fl oz (90 ml) vodka
⅓ fl oz (10 ml) rose water
1 cinnamon stick for garnish

Half fill a cocktail shaker with ice. Add vodka and rose water. Stir and strain into a chilled martini glass. Garnish with cinnamon stick.

Hazelnut martini

ice cubes
3 fl oz (90 ml) vodka
½ fl oz (15 ml) Frangelico
6 sliced (flaked) almonds, toasted for garnish

Half fill a cocktail shaker with ice. Add vodka and Frangelico. Stir and strain into a chilled martini glass. Garnish with almonds.

Apple martini

ice cubes
2 fl oz (60 ml) vodka
2 fl oz (60 ml) Calvados
1 thin slice apple for garnish

Half fill a cocktail shaker with ice. Add vodka and Calvados. Stir and strain into a chilled large martini glass. Garnish with apple slice.

Left: Rosewater and cinnamon martini (front), Hazelnut martini (back)

martinis

Berry martini

ice cubes
2 fl oz (60 ml) vodka
1 fl oz (30 ml) eau-de-vie framboise sauvage or eau-de-vie de fraise
1 fresh raspberry or strawberry for garnish

Half fill a cocktail shaker with ice. Add vodka and eau-de-vie. Stir and strain into a chilled martini glass. Garnish with raspberry or strawberry.

Audience martini

ice cubes
3 fl oz (90 ml) gin
dash of orange bitters
splash of blood orange juice
1 grapefruit twist for garnish

Half fill a cocktail shaker with ice. Add gin, bitters and juice. Stir and strain into a chilled martini glass. Garnish with grapefruit twist.

Honey martini

ice cubes
2 fl oz (60 ml) vodka
1 fl oz (30 ml) Old Krupnik
1 tangerine (mandarin orange) twist for garnish

Half fill a cocktail shaker with ice. Add vodka and Old Krupnik. Stir and strain into a chilled martini glass. Garnish with tangerine twist.

Vanilla martini

ice cubes
2 fl oz (60 ml) vodka
½ fl oz (15 ml) Licor 43
1 vanilla bean for garnish

Half fill a cocktail shaker with ice. Add vodka and Licor 43. Stir and strain into a chilled martini glass. Place vanilla bean in martini or resting across glass.

Right: Audience martini

martinis

Sake martini

ice cubes
1 fl oz (30 ml) sake
1 fl oz (30 ml) vodka
dash of gin
1 slice cucumber
for garnish

Half fill a cocktail shaker with ice. Add sake, vodka and gin. Stir and strain into a chilled martini glass. Garnish with cucumber slice.

Beetle

ice cubes
1 fl oz (30 ml) vodka
1 fl oz (30 ml) Chartreuse
½ fl oz (15 ml) Triple Sec

Half fill a cocktail shaker with ice. Add vodka, Chartreuse and Triple Sec. Stir and strain into a chilled martini glass.

Lemon warhead

ice cubes
3 fl oz (90 ml)
Absolut Citron vodka
dash of angostura bitters
1 lemon twist for garnish

Half fill a cocktail shaker with ice. Add vodka and bitters. Stir and strain into a chilled martini glass. Garnish with lemon twist.

Strange keys

ice cubes
2 orange quarters
2 fl oz (60 ml) sloe gin
½ fl oz (15 ml) Cognac

Half fill a cocktail shaker with ice. Squeeze orange into shaker. Add sloe gin and Cognac. Stir and strain into a chilled martini glass.

Watermelon martini

ice cubes
1½ fl oz (45 ml) vodka
2 fl oz (60 ml)
watermelon juice
dash of sugar syrup
1 small slice watermelon
for garnish

Half fill a cocktail shaker with ice. Add vodka, watermelon juice and sugar syrup. Stir and strain into a chilled martini glass. Garnish with watermelon slice.

blended cocktails

"…every good quality is noxious if unmixed."
— *Ralph Waldo Emerson*

Now there's a plea for a blended cocktail if ever there was one! Emerson knew a thing or two about quality, even if he may not have been thinking about cocktails on this occasion. But his observation is no less applicable: the freshest of fruit and good-quality ice are essential for the success of a blended cocktail.

In fact, blending is one of the easiest methods of mixing a cocktail. All you do is combine ice cubes, fruit, alcohol and, sometimes cream, in a blender.

A blender is essential for these cocktails. If you don't already have one, be sure to invest in a good quality model. One that's strong enough to crush ice (look for one with a 400–500-watt motor); check the user manual to be sure it's suitable for this use.

Choose a blender with a glass container. That way you can enjoy watching the colors come together. And make sure it has a tight-fitting lid, so you don't end up with more liquid on the floor than in the glass. Ideally, it should also have a pouring spout or lip.

One last tip on the subject of ice: don't use tap water, which can contain any number of vile-tasting "purifiers," or cubes that have served time in the same cell as other foods and so have absorbed some of their neighbors' odors. Good-quality bottled water, preferably spring water, is best. Freeze it into cubes as close to cocktail preparation time as possible. You won't believe what a difference it makes to the taste.

blended cocktails

Grand mango

1 fl oz (30 ml) mango purée
1 fl oz (30 ml) Campari
1½ fl oz (15 ml) Grand Marnier
½ cup (2½ oz/75 g) ice cubes

Pour mango purée into a chilled cocktail or martini glass. In a blender, combine Campari, Grand Marnier and ice. Blend and pour over mango purée.

Candy pop

1 cup (5 oz/150 g) ice cubes
½ fl oz (15 ml) peach schnapps
½ fl oz (15 ml) apple schnapps
½ fl oz (15 ml) strawberry liqueur
2 fl oz (60 ml) lemon juice
1 fl oz (30 ml) orange juice
1 fresh strawberry and 1 lime twist for garnish

In a blender, combine ice, schnapps, liqueur and juices. Blend and pour into a chilled cocktail or martini glass. Garnish with a strawberry and lime twist.

Right: Grand mango

blended cocktails

Slivovitz plum daiquiri

½ cup (2½ oz/75 g) ice cubes
2 fl oz (60 ml) slivovitz
⅓ fl oz (10 ml) Cointreau
⅓ fl oz (10 ml) lemon juice
3 fresh plums, peeled and pitted, or 3 canned plums, drained
1 fresh strawberry for garnish

In a blender, combine ice, slivovitz, Cointreau, lemon juice and plums. Blend and pour into a chilled cocktail or martini glass. Garnish with strawberry.

Berry splice

½ cup (2½ oz/75 g) ice cubes
½ fl oz (15 ml) Baileys Irish Cream
½ fl oz (15 ml) framboise
½ fl oz (15 ml) crème de cacao
½ fl oz (15 ml) Kahlúa
5 fresh strawberries, hulled
¼ cup (2 fl oz/60 ml) half-and-half cream (half milk, half cream)
1 fl oz (30 ml) crème de mûre

In a blender, combine ice, Baileys, framboise, crème de cacao, Kahlúa, 4 strawberries and cream. Blend. Pour crème de mûre into a chilled cocktail glass. Pour blended mixture over the back of a spoon to layer it over crème de mûre. Garnish with remaining strawberry.

Left: Berry splice

blended cocktails

Honeydew and kiwifruit daiquiri

½ cup (3 oz/90 g) chopped honeydew melon
1 kiwifruit, peeled and chopped
2 fl oz (60 ml) Bacardi white rum
½ fl oz (15 ml) lemon juice
½ fl oz (15 ml) sugar syrup
sugar and 1 fresh mint sprig for garnish

In a blender, combine melon, kiwifruit, rum, lemon juice and sugar syrup. Blend and pour into a sugar-rimmed margarita or large martini glass. Garnish with mint sprig.

Caper and chili juice

6 ice cubes
2 fl oz (60 ml) vodka
1 small fresh red chili, seeded
1 small ripe tomato, seeded
dash of Worcestershire sauce
dash of Tabasco sauce
6 capers
ground white pepper and 1 stick of cucumber for garnish

In a blender, combine ice cubes, vodka, chili, tomato, sauces and capers. Blend and pour into a white pepper-rimmed shot glass. Garnish with cucumber stick.

Right: Caper and chili juice

blended cocktails

Left: Banana and pineapple refresher

Banana fizz

½ banana, peeled and chopped
½ cup (2½ oz/75 g) ice cubes
1 fl oz (30 ml) vodka
½ fl oz (15 ml) banana liqueur
½ fl oz (15 ml) lemon juice
lemonade or soda water, chilled (optional)
1 fresh flower for garnish

In a blender, combine banana, ice, vodka, banana liqueur and lemon juice. Blend and pour into a chilled cocktail or large martini glass. Top with lemonade or soda water, if you like. Garnish with fresh flower.

Banana and pineapple refresher

5 fresh strawberries, hulled, plus 1 slice strawberry for garnish
dash of sugar syrup
½ cup (2½ oz/75 g) ice cubes
½ fl oz (15 ml) white rum
½ cup (3 oz/90 g) chopped pineapple
½ banana, peeled and chopped
1 lime, peeled
2 fresh mint leaves

In a blender, combine strawberries and sugar syrup. Blend and pour into a chilled cocktail or large martini glass. Rinse blender and place ice, white rum, pineapple, banana, limes and mint in it. Blend and pour over strawberry purée. Garnish with strawberry slice.

blended cocktails

Sgroppino

1 scoop lemon sorbet
2 fl oz (60 ml) prosecco
1 lemon slice for garnish

In a blender, combine sorbet and prosecco. Blend and pour into a chilled old-fashioned glass. Garnish with lemon slice.

Golden banana

½ cup (2½ oz/75 g) ice cubes
2 fl oz (60 ml) Jamaican rum
½ banana, peeled and chopped
1 teaspoon vanilla extract
1 lemon wedge for garnish

In a blender, combine ice, rum, banana and vanilla. Blend and pour into a chilled cocktail or martini glass. Garnish with lemon wedge.

Right: Sgroppino

blended cocktails

Left: Boysenberry daiquiri (back), Strawberry daiquiri (front)

Berry surprise

½ cup (2½ oz/75 g) ice cubes
1 fl oz (30 ml) vodka
½ fl oz (15 ml) raspberry liqueur
1 fl oz (30 ml) grapefruit juice
1 fl oz (30 ml) cranberry juice
1 fl oz (30 ml) blackcurrant juice
¼ fl oz (7½ ml) blue curaçao
3 fresh or canned peach wedges, plus 1 peach wedge for garnish

In a blender, combine ice, vodka, raspberry liqueur, juices, blue curaçao and 3 peach wedges. Blend and pour into a chilled cocktail or martini glass. Garnish with remaining peach wedge.

Fruit daiquiris

½ cup (2½ oz/75 g) ice cubes
1 cup (4 oz/125 g) chopped fresh mango or banana or 1 cup (4 oz/125 g) whole strawberries, raspberries, lychees or boysenberries
2 fl oz (60 ml) Bacardi white rum
1 fl oz (30 ml) flavored liqueur (specific to fruit chosen)
⅓ fl oz (10 ml) lemon juice
fresh fruit slices or berries for garnish

In a blender, combine ice, fruit, rum, liqueur and lemon juice. Blend and pour into a chilled cocktail or martini glass. Garnish with slices of fruit or berries.

blended cocktails

Coconut holiday

1 cup (5 oz/150 g) ice cubes
1½ fl oz (45 ml) dark rum
1 fl oz (30 ml) pineapple juice
1 fl oz (30 ml) orange juice
1 fl oz (30 ml) cranberry juice
1 fl oz (30 ml) coconut cream
fresh pineapple leaves for garnish

In a blender, combine ice, rum, juices and coconut cream. Blend and pour into a highball glass. Garnish with pineapple leaves.

Pear daiquiri

1 cup (5 oz/150 g) ice cubes
1 fl oz (30 ml) Bacardi white rum
1 fl oz (30 ml) Poire William
½ poached or canned pear
1 teaspoon lemon juice
1 fresh flower for garnish

In a blender, combine ice, rum, Poire William, pear and lemon juice. Blend and pour into a chilled cocktail or martini glass. Garnish with flower.

Right: Mango daiquiri, see previous page for recipe

crushed cocktails

"My critic has muddled it together in a most extraordinary manner."
—*J. H. Newman*

The preparation of so-called "crushed" cocktails or "stick drinks" gives you an opportunity to employ that most unappetizing of verbs, "to muddle."

"I'll just go and muddle the mint leaves and sugar," you can tell your bemused guests, as you slip behind the bar or head for the kitchen to prepare that mint julep. Professional mixologists, of course, are never caught without their muddler—a wooden stick with a flattened end—used to mash ingredients together to slowly release their flavors.

If you have got a muddler, you'll appreciate how its wooden end won't scratch the glass. If you don't have one, use the back of a spoon, the end of a rolling pin or a pestle to crush the ingredients against the base and side of the serving glass, not forgetting to first wrap a towel around the glass to prevent it breaking in mid-muddle. Use a mortar and pestle if you're preparing more than one drink of this kind.

Your blender can provide crushed ice. If it's not up to the job, try this: put the ice cubes in a sealable plastic bag, cover with a towel, and bash with a meat tenderizer. Don't apply too much force, though, or you'll tear the towel. Unwrap, unzip and transfer to the waiting glasses.

Crushed cocktails are generally served in old-fashioned or highball glasses.

crushed cocktails

Apple man

½ apple, peeled, cored and chopped, plus 1 apple wedge for garnish
ice cubes
1 fl oz (30 ml) vodka
1 fl oz (30 ml) gin
1 fl oz (30 ml) Calvados
soda water, chilled

Put chopped apple in a highball glass and muddle until crushed. Fill glass with ice and add vodka, gin and Calvados. Top with soda water and stir well. Garnish with apple wedge.

Tangerine cooler

6 fresh mint leaves
1 sugar cube
1 tangerine (mandarin orange), cut into wedges
ice cubes
1 fl oz (30 ml) Absolut Citron vodka
1 fl oz (30 ml) cranberry juice, chilled

In a highball glass, combine mint leaves and sugar cube. Muddle until sugar is crushed, then add tangerine wedges. Muddle until juice is extracted. Fill glass with ice. Add vodka and cranberry juice and stir.

Blood orange crush

crushed ice
1½ fl oz (45 ml) Campari
½ fl oz (15 ml) Cointreau
blood orange juice, chilled
ruby red grapefruit juice
wedge ruby red grapefruit
for garnish

Fill an old-fashioned glass with crushed ice. Add Campari and Cointreau. Top with equal amounts of blood orange juice and grapefruit juice. If desired, garnish with wedge of ruby red grapefruit.

Pine lime crush

crushed ice
4 lime wedges
2 fl oz (60 ml) vodka
pineapple juice, chilled

Fill an old-fashioned glass with crushed ice. Squeeze lime wedges over ice then put lime peels into glass. Add vodka, top with pineapple juice and stir.

crushed cocktails

Caipiroska

1 lime, cut into eighths
3 sugar cubes
ice cubes
2 fl oz (60 ml) vodka

In a highball glass, combine lime wedges and sugar. Muddle until juice is extracted and sugar is crushed. Fill glass with ice, pour vodka in, and stir.

Berry caipiroska

2 lime quarters
3 fresh strawberries, hulled
2 fresh blueberries
2 fresh raspberries
4 ruby red grapefruit juice ice cubes
2 fl oz (60 ml) vodka
½ fl oz (15 ml) framboise

In an old-fashioned glass, combine lime quarters, 2 strawberries, blueberries and raspberries. Muddle until berries are crushed. Add grapefruit juice ice cubes. Pour vodka and framboise over ice and stir well. Garnish with remaining strawberry.

Grapefruit caipiroska

2 grapefruit wedges, chopped and peel removed
2 lime wedges
ice cubes
1½ fl oz (45 ml) Absolut Kurant vodka
½ fl oz (15 ml) crème de mûre
ruby red grapefruit juice, chilled
1 grapefruit twist for garnish

In an old-fashioned glass, combine grapefruit flesh and lime wedges. Muddle until juice is extracted. Fill glass with ice, and add vodka and crème de mûre. Top with grapefruit juice and stir well. Garnish with grapefruit twist.

Passion fruit caipiroska

1 lime, quartered
pulp of 1 passionfruit
ice cubes
2 fl oz (60 ml) vodka
1 fl oz (30 ml) passionfruit liqueur
1 fresh flower for garnish

Put lime quarters in an old-fashioned glass and muddle until juice is extracted. Add passionfruit pulp and fill glass with ice. Pour vodka and passionfruit liqueur over ice and stir. Garnish with fresh flower.

**Variation:
Lychee caipiroska**
Use fresh lychee and lychee licqueur in place of passionfruit and passionfruit liqueur

crushed cocktails

Caiperol

1 lime, cut into eighths
3 sugar cubes
ice cubes
2 fl oz (60 ml) Aperol

Put lime wedges and sugar into a highball glass. Muddle until juice is extracted and sugar is crushed. Fill glass with ice. Add Aperol and stir

Eau de Coing

crushed ice
1 fl oz (30 ml) quince liqueur
1 fl oz (30 ml) Frangelico
blood orange juice, chilled
fresh mint leaves for garnish

Fill a highball glass with crushed ice. Add quince liqueur and Frangelico. Top with blood orange juice and stir. Garnish with mint leaves..

Ginger mojito

1 teaspoon grated fresh ginger
1 lime, cut into wedges
6 fresh mint leaves, plus extra mint leaves for garnish
1 teaspoon sugar
ice cubes
2 fl oz (60 ml) golden rum
soda water, chilled

In an old-fashioned glass, combine ginger, lime, 6 mint leaves and sugar. Muddle until juice is extracted and sugar is crushed. Fill glass with ice and pour in rum. Top with soda water and stir well. Garnish with extra mint leaves.

Jaggard crush

crushed ice
4 lime quarters
1 fl oz (30 ml) Jaggard Original
1 fl oz (30 ml) Cointreau
½ fl oz (15 ml) Absolut Citron vodka
1/2 fl oz (15 ml) Absolut Kurant vodka
ruby red grapefruit juice, chilled
1 ruby red grapefruit wedge for garnish

Fill a highball glass with crushed ice. Squeeze lime quarters over ice then put lime peels in glass. Add Jaggard, Cointreau and vodkas. Top with grapefruit juice. Garnish with grapefruit wedge.

Gin club

4 fresh mint leaves, plus
extra mint leaves for garnish
3 sugar cubes
ice cubes
2 fl oz (60 ml) gin
½ fl oz (15 ml) Aperol

In a highball glass, combine
4 mint leaves and sugar.
Muddle until sugar is
crushed. Fill glass with ice.
Add gin and Aperol, and
stir. Garnish with extra
mint leaves.

built cocktails

"A successful marriage is an edifice that must be rebuilt every day."
—*André Maurois*

In our case, an edifice of ice—whole or crushed—alcohol, juice and decoration. As for rebuilding it every day … all you need to do is quote André Maurois and you have the perfect excuse for creating one of these fabulous thirst-quenchers day in, day out.

Yes, built cocktails are meant for slaking the parched throat, rather than for slow sipping. And don't they look good! The Japanese say that food should look good as well as taste good. So should cocktails, and here's proof.

Built cocktails are among the simplest around and require the minimum of equipment. All you do is take a highball or old-fashioned glass, fill it with ice (from bottled water, of course), then the liquid ingredients. Give the lot a slow stir with a long bar spoon so the flavors blend gently with each other. As a final touch, let your imagination go wild and decorate the drink with garnishes of fruit, lime or orange zest, even pineapple leaves.

built cocktails

Ginger melon

ice cubes
1½ fl oz (45 ml)
Absolut Citron vodka
½ fl oz (15 ml) Cointreau
½ fl oz (15 ml) ginger liqueur
3 fl oz (90 ml)
watermelon juice
1 orange wedge for garnish

Fill a highball glass with ice. Add vodka, Cointreau, ginger liqueur and watermelon juice. Stir and garnish with orange wedge.

Pisco sour

ice cubes
2 fl oz (60 ml) pisco
2 fl oz (60 ml) lime juice
dash of sugar syrup
1 lime twist for garnish

Fill an old-fashioned glass with ice. Add pisco, lime juice and sugar syrup, and stir. Garnish with lime twist.

Right: Ginger melon

Ginger 'n' orange

ice cubes
3 orange wedges
fresh orange juice, chilled
½ fl oz (15 ml) fresh ginger juice
1 fl oz (30 ml) vodka
ginger ale, chilled
1 fresh mint leaf for garnish

In an old-fashioned glass, combine ice and orange wedges. Fill glass one-third full with orange juice. Add ginger juice and vodka. Top with ginger ale, and stir. Garnish with mint leaf.

built cocktails

Tiberian sun

ice cubes
1½ fl oz (45 ml)
Absolut Citron vodka
½ fl oz (15 ml) Cointreau
½ fl oz (15 ml)
crème de mûre
1 teaspoon puréed
boysenberries
pear juice, chilled
2 lime wedges for garnish

Fill a highball glass with ice. Add vodka, Cointreau, crème de mûre and boysenberry purée. Top with pear juice and stir. Garnish with lime wedges.

Soda nut

ice cubes
½ fl oz (15 ml) amaretto
2 fl oz (60 ml) fresh
orange juice
2 fl oz (60 ml) chilled
soda water
1 orange twist for garnish

Fill a highball glass with ice. Add amaretto and orange juice. Top with soda water and stir. Garnish with orange twist.

built cocktails

Lifesaver

ice cubes
1 fl oz (30 ml)
raspberry liqueur
1 fl oz (30 ml) gin
2 fl oz (60 ml) guava nectar
dash of angostura bitters
pineapple leaves for garnish

Fill a highball glass with ice. Add raspberry liqueur, gin, guava nectar and bitters. Stir and garnish with pineapple leaves.

Sunshine

crushed ice
1 fl oz (30 ml) dark rum
½ fl oz (15 ml) Cointreau
1 fl oz (30 ml) apricot nectar
1 fl oz (30 ml) tangerine (mandarin orange) juice
¼ fl oz (7½ ml) lime juice
1 orange twist for garnish

Fill a large martini glass with crushed ice. Add rum, Cointreau, apricot nectar and juices. Stir and garnish with orange twist.

King

ice cubes
1 fl oz (30 ml) brandy
½ fl oz (15 ml) lemon juice
½ fl oz (15 ml) lime juice
soda water, chilled
1 lime wedge for garnish

Fill a highball glass with ice. Add brandy and juices. Top with soda water and stir. Garnish with lime wedge.

Blackberry emergency

ice cubes
½ fl oz (15 ml) Absolut Citron vodka
½ fl oz (15 ml) Absolut Kurant vodka
⅓ fl oz (10 ml) crème de cassis
⅓ fl oz (10 ml) Triple Sec
¼ fl oz (7½ ml) fresh lime juice
cranberry juice, chilled
1 lime twist for garnish

Fill a highball glass with ice. Add vodkas, crème de cassis, Triple Sec and lime juice. Top with cranberry juice and stir. Garnish with lime twist.

Right: Lifesaver

Wild strawberries

ice cubes
3 fresh strawberries, hulled
1 fl oz (30 ml)
fraise des bois
1 fl oz (30 ml) light rum
squeeze of lemon juice
soda water or
lemonade, chilled

Fill a highball glass with ice. Add strawberries, fraise des bois, rum and lemon juice. Top with soda water or lemonade and stir.

built cocktails

Gingerene

crushed ice
1 fl oz (30 ml) gin
1 fl oz (30 ml) ginger liqueur
1 fl oz (30 ml) golden rum
3 lime juice ice cubes
1 fl oz (30 ml) tangerine
(mandarin orange) juice
1 tangerine (mandarin
orange) wedge for garnish

Fill a large martini glass with crushed ice. Add gin, ginger liqueur, rum, lime juice ice cubes and tangerine juice and stir. Garnish with tangerine wedge.

Cranberry and apple sour

ice cubes
1 fl oz (30 ml)
apple schnapps
1 fl oz (30 ml) lime juice
2 fl oz (60 ml)
cranberry juice
splash of Bacardi 151 rum
1 lime wedge for garnish

Fill a highball glass with ice. Add schnapps, juices and rum and stir. Garnish with lime wedge.

built cocktails

Napoleon

ice cubes
1 fl oz (30 ml)
Mandarin Napoleon
¼ fl oz (7½ ml) Cointreau
1 fl oz (30 ml) lime juice
3 orange juice ice cubes
1 lime twist for garnish

Fill a highball glass with ice. Add Mandarin Napoleon, Cointreau, lime juice and orange juice ice cubes and stir. Garnish with lime twist.

Citrus fountain

crushed ice
2 fl oz (60 ml)
Absolut Mandarin vodka
1 fl oz (30 ml) Cognac
1 fl oz (30 ml) grapefruit juice
1 fl oz (30 ml) orange juice
1 fl oz (30 ml) lime juice
1 grapefruit wedge
for garnish

Fill a large martini glass with crushed ice. Add vodka, Cognac and juices and stir. Garnish with grapefruit wedge.

Ginger and mandarin sea breeze

ice cubes
½ fl oz (15 ml) ginger liqueur
½ fl oz (15 ml)
Absolut Mandarin vodka
3 cranberry juice ice cubes
1 fl oz (30 ml) grapefruit juice
1 lime wedge for garnish

Fill a highball glass with ice. Add ginger liqueur, vodka, cranberry juice ice cubes and grapefruit juice and stir. Garnish with lime wedge.

Soda and citrus

ice cubes
1 fl oz (30 ml)
peach schnapps
1 fl oz (30 ml) lime juice
1 fl oz (30 ml) grapefruit juice
soda water, chilled
1 peach wedge for garnish

Fill a highball glass with ice. Add schnapps and juices. Top with soda water and stir. Garnish with peach wedge.

Guava vogue

ice cubes
1 fl oz (30 ml) tequila
1 fl oz (30 ml) Cointreau
1 fl oz (30 ml) guava juice
1 fl oz (30 ml) lime juice
soda water, chilled
1 papaya wedge and
lime zest for garnish

Fill a highball glass with ice. Add tequila, Cointreau and juices. Top with soda water and stir. Garnish with papaya wedge and lime zest.

shaken and strained cocktails

"When taken, to be well shaken."
—*George Coleman the Younger, from* The Newcastle Apothecary

We've all heard James Bond's preference for "shaken, not stirred." Shaken cocktails are by far the most impressive and fun to watch. Remember the movie *Cocktail* with Tom Cruise and Bryan Brown?

But why restrict your enjoyment to the silver screen or watching cocktail-bartenders hurling shakers about like circus stars. You can get more kicks by doing it yourself at home or at a party. Just make sure the lid's firmly attached!

Here are the rules:
1. Keep the shaker, whether metal or glass, in the freezer until you need it.
2. Fill the shaker with ice cubes before you add your chosen cocktail ingredients.
3. Shaking means vigorous blending, so shake with a good, steady rhythm. Put on some music and shake to the beat.
4. Shake only one drink at a time. That way you get to repeat the performance. You never know—there might be a talent scout somewhere in the audience.
5. Remove the lid with a flourish and strain the drink into a chilled cocktail glass. If your shaker comes with a strainer, use that. If not, here's your chance to use that professional strainer some hopeful friend gave you last birthday.
6. Garnish your masterpiece, sit back and enjoy. Or present it to your guests before whipping one up "for the cook."

shaken and strained cocktails

Raspberry sourgear

ice cubes
1 fl oz (30 ml) gin
½ fl oz (15 ml) Monin Lime
natural mineral water with orange juice
½ fl oz (15 ml) raspberry liqueur

Fill a highball glass and a cocktail shaker with ice. Add gin and Monin Lime to shaker. Shake and strain into ice-filled glass. Top with mineral water with orange juice. Top with raspberry liqueur.

Cherry tree

ice cubes
1 fl oz (30 ml) cherry liqueur
1 fl oz (30 ml) Calvados
1 fl oz (30 ml) lemon juice
1 fl oz (30 ml) lime juice

Fill a highball glass and a cocktail shaker with ice. Add cherry liqueur, Calvados and juices to shaker. Shake and strain into ice-filled glass.

Blood berries

ice cubes
½ fl oz (15 ml) Chambord
½ fl oz (15 ml) vodka
1 fl oz (30 ml) blood orange juice
1 fl oz (30 ml) cranberry juice

Fill a cocktail shaker with ice. Add Chambord, vodka and juices. Shake and strain into a large martini glass.

Tangerine sour

ice cubes
2 fl oz (60 ml) pisco
1 fl oz (30 ml) tangerine (mandarin orange) juice
1 fl oz (30 ml) lime juice
dash of lightly beaten egg white
1 tangorino (mandarin orange) wedge for garnish

Fill a cocktail shaker with ice cubes. Add pisco, juices and egg white. Shake and strain into a large martini glass. Garnish with tangerine wedge.

Right: Raspberry Collins (front), Raspberry sourgear (back)

Raspberry Collins

ice cubes
2 fl oz (60 ml) vodka
½ fl oz (15 ml) lemon juice
1 fl oz (30 ml) framboise
2 teaspoons raspberry purée
soda water, chilled

Fill a highball glass and cocktail shaker with ice. Add vodka, lemon juice, framboise and raspberry purée to shaker. Shake and strain into ice-filled glass. Top with soda.

Strawberry Hills

ice cubes
1½ fl oz (45 ml) tequila
½ fl oz (15 ml) Triple Sec
½ fl oz (15 ml) lime juice
2 teaspoons strawberry purée
dash of strawberry liqueur

Fill a cocktail shaker with ice. Add tequila, Triple Sec, lime juice, strawberry purée and strawberry liqueur. Shake and strain into a cocktail glass or wineglass.

shaken and strained cocktails

Peach and apricot shaker

ice cubes
1 fl oz (30 ml) gin
1 fl oz (30 ml) Cointreau
1 fl oz (30 ml) apricot nectar
1 fl oz (30 ml) peach nectar
½ fl oz (15 ml) grapefruit juice
sugar for garnish

Fill a cocktail shaker with ice. Add gin, Cointreau, nectars and juice. Shake and strain into sugar-rimmed large martini glass.

Margarita no. 5

ice cubes
2 fl oz (60 ml) tequila
1 fl oz (30 ml) Cointreau
⅓ fl oz (10 ml) lemon juice
½ fl oz (15 ml) ruby red grapefruit juice
½ fl oz (15 ml) orange juice
½ fl oz (15 ml) lime juice
½ fl oz (15 ml) blood orange juice
dash of lightly beaten egg white
sugar for garnish

Fill a cocktail shaker with ice. Add tequila, Cointreau, juices and egg white. Shake and strain into a sugar-rimmed large martini or margarita glass.

Spitfire

ice cubes
2 fl oz (60 ml) gin
1 fl oz (30 ml) Cointreau
2 fl oz (60 ml) ruby red grapefruit juice
dash of angostura bitters
dash of sugar syrup
dash of lightly beaten egg white

Fill a cocktail shaker with ice. Add gin, Cointreau, grapefruit juice, bitters, sugar syrup and egg white. Shake and strain into a large martini glass.

Scoloco

ice cubes
2 fl oz (60 ml) pisco
½ fl oz (15 ml) Cointreau
½ fl oz (15 ml) Aperol
½ fl oz (15 ml) lime juice
½ fl oz (15 ml) lemon juice

Fill an old-fashioned glass and a cocktail shaker with ice. Add pisco, Cointreau, Aperol and juices to shaker. Shake and strain into ice-filled glass.

shaken and strained cocktails

Blanc

ice cubes
1 fl oz (30 ml) gin
1 fl oz (30 ml) lime juice
1 fl oz (30 ml) Cointreau
1 fl oz (30 ml) Lillet Blanc
1 lime wedge for garnish

Fill a cocktail shaker with ice. Add gin, juice, Cointreau and Lillet Blanc. Shake and strain into a large martini glass. Garnish with lime wedge.

Pimms and green tea refresher

long thin slices cucumber (made with a vegetable peeler)
ice cubes
2 fl oz (60 ml) Pimms
½ fl oz (15 ml) Monin Lime
1 cup (8 fl oz/250 ml) cold green tea

Arrange cucumber slices in a highball glass. Fill glass and a cocktail shaker with ice cubes. Add Pimms, Monin Lime and cold tea to shaker. Shake and strain into ice-filled glass.

Verbs

ice cubes
1 fl oz (30 ml) lemon verbena liqueur
1 fl oz (30 ml) pisco
2 fl oz (60 ml) blood orange juice
1 orange wedge for garnish

Fill a cocktail shaker with ice. Add lemon verbena liqueur, pisco and orange juice. Shake and strain into a large martini glass. Garnish with orange wedge.

Green fairy

ice cubes
1 fl oz (30 ml) absinthe or Pernod
1 fl oz (30 ml) Cointreau
1 fl oz (30 ml) lime juice
1 teaspoon honey
1 orange slice for garnish

Fill a cocktail shaker with ice. Add absinthe or Pernod, Cointreau, juice and honey. Shake and strain into Champagne saucer. Garnish with orange slice.

Sour morning

1 long strip orange zest
ice cubes
½ fl oz (15 ml) vodka
dash of angostura bitters
2 fl oz (60 ml)
grapefruit juice
2 fl oz (60 ml)
ruby red grapefruit juice
2 fl oz (60 ml)
blood orange juice
1 fl oz (30 ml) lemon juice
1 fl oz (30 ml) lime juice

Curl orange zest around the inside of an old-fashioned glass. Fill glass and a cocktail shaker with ice cubes. Add bitters, vodka and juices to shaker. Shake and strain into an ice-filled glass.

Nonalcoholic cocktails

"…a place wherein all pleasant fruits do flow."
—Thomas Campion 1567–1620

If you want the fun without the hangover there are loads of nonalcoholic cocktails that look just like the real thing and still allow you to drive home safely.

And because you can dress up these combos with colorful garnishes in glasses with frosted rims, they're sure to be popular with kids keen to strut their sophistication. Just dip the rim of the glass in beaten egg white, then sugar or salt, before filling it up with freshly juiced fruits or vegetables of choice. Do you know a sneakier way of getting them to take their vitamins?

Nonalcoholic cocktails

Tutti frutti

6 fresh strawberries, hulled
½ cup (2½ oz/75 g) ice cubes
½ fl oz (15 ml) apricot juice
½ fl oz (15 ml) pineapple juice
½ fl oz (15 ml) ruby red grapefruit juice
½ fl oz (15 ml) cranberry juice
½ fl oz (15 ml) orange juice
½ fl oz (15 ml) lemon juice
½ mango, peeled, cut from pit and chopped
1 ruby red grapefruit wedge for garnish

Put strawberries in a blender and purée. Pour into a Champagne saucer. Rinse blender and add ice, juices and mango. Purée and pour over strawberry purée. Garnish with grapefruit wedge.

Crenshaw

ice cubes
2 fl oz (60 ml) cranberry juice
1 fl oz (30 ml) ruby red grapefruit juice
dash of pineapple juice
½ fl oz (15 ml) sour cherry syrup
dash of angostura bitters
1 orange wedge for garnish

Fill a highball glass with ice. Add juices, syrup and bitters, and stir. Squeeze orange wedge into a glass and garnish glass with peel.

Tropicana

1 cup (5 oz/150 g) ice cubes
½ cup (4 fl oz/125 ml) pineapple juice
½ fl oz (15 ml) lychee juice
¼ cup (1½ oz/45 g) chopped papaya (pawpaw)
½ cup (3 oz/90 g) chopped mango
2 fresh mint leaves for garnish

In a blender, combine ice, juices, papaya and mango. Purée and pour into a large cocktail or martini glass. Garnish with mint leaves.

Strawfruit

1 kiwifruit, peeled and coarsely chopped
3 fresh strawberries, hulled
ice cubes
½ fl oz (15 ml) apricot nectar
½ fl oz (15 ml) cranberry juice
soda water or lemonade, chilled

In a glass, combine kiwifruit and 2 strawberries. Muddle until crushed. Fill glass with ice. Add apricot nectar and cranberry juice. Top with soda water and stir. Garnish with remaining strawberry.

Ginger and peach punch

1 cup (5 oz/150 g) ice cubes
2 cups (16 fl oz/500 ml) peach nectar, chilled
¼ cup (2 fl oz/60 ml) lime juice
2 peaches, peeled, pitted and sliced
¼ cup (2 fl oz/60 ml) ginger syrup
4 cups (32 fl oz/1 L) ginger beer, chilled
1 lime, thinly sliced, and 8 fresh mint leaves for garnish

In a large, attractive glass bowl, combine ice cubes, peach nectar, lime juice, peaches, ginger syrup and ginger beer and stir. Garnish with lime slices and mint leaves.

Serves 6

Affogato

1 scoop good-quality vanilla ice cream
⅓ cup (3 fl oz/90 ml) hot espresso coffee
1 fl oz (30 ml) Kahlúa

Put ice cream in a heatproof glass. Pour hot espresso coffee and kahlúa over ice cream.

hot drinks

"Nothing says romance like a hot toddy on a cool morning."
—www.savannahsays.com

Corretto

¼ cup (2 fl oz/60 ml) half-and-half cream (half milk, half cream)
½ fl oz (15 ml) amaretto
½ cup (4 fl oz/125 ml) hot strong espresso coffee

Using a coffee machine steam wand, froth half-and-half cream and amaretto until hot. Or heat in a small saucepan over a low heat, stirring constantly, until hot, about 1 minute. Pour hot coffee into a heatproof glass. Pour hot cream mixture over and serve immediately.

Mulled wine

5 sugar cubes
4 cups (32 fl oz/1 L) red wine
2 cinnamon sticks
1 strip lemon zest
1 fl oz (30 ml) curaçao

In a nonreactive saucepan, combine sugar cubes, wine, cinnamon sticks and lemon zest. Place over medium heat and cook until a gray scum appears on the surface of the wine. Do not boil. Remove pan from heat and skim scum from surface. Stir in curaçao and let stand for 5 minutes. Strain and serve warm.

Serves 4

Winter warmer

1 fl oz (30 ml) Scotch whisky
1 fl oz (30 ml) lemon juice
1 tablespoon honey
1 teaspoon green tea leaves
1 cup (8 fl oz/250 ml) boiling water

In a heatproof glass, combine Scotch, lemon juice and honey. Put tea in a teapot and pour boiling water over. Cover and steep. Strain tea and pour into glass. Stir and serve.

Hot drinks are the great pretenders of the cocktail world. They taste great and warm you up after a hard day. Apparently, they don't really heat up much more than your mouth and throat, but hey, who cares? The steam rising, spreading all kinds of delicious smells, the relaxing effect of warm liquid slipping down your throat…It might be only theater, but it certainly deserves a round of applause.

glossary

absinthe: An anise-flavored liqueur that is illegal in the US because it is based on the wormwood plant. Pernod should be substituted where absinthe is unavailable.

Absolut Mandarin/Citron/Kurant: Flavored vodkas from the Absolut brand.

amaretto: A liqueur flavored with almonds, apricot kernels and seeds.

angostura bitters: An aromatic mix of a variety of botanicals; the seeds, roots, leaves, fruit, bark and stems of various flora in an alcoholic base.

Aperol: An Italian aperitif similar to Campari and tasting of burnt oranges.

Baileys Irish Cream: A rich, sweet liqueur made with cream and Irish whiskey; Baileys was the first brand to make it.

Bacardi: A well-known brand of rum with many varieties, including white rum and Bacardi 151 rum; see also Rum.

Bénédictine: An aromatic herbal liqueur originally invented by a Benedictine monk in the sixteenth century.

berry-infused vodka: Vodka that has had berries soaking in it until the flavor imbues the spirit; see also Flavored spirits, in Ingredients.

blue curaçao: An orange-flavored liqueur, see also Curaçao.

bourbon: A type of whiskey distilled from grains (mostly maize but also barley and rye) and aged in oak barrels, and available in various ages and blends.

brandy: A spirit made from distilling wine, fermented fruit juice or fruit pulp, brandy is also known as eau-de-vie; its quality usually depends on its age.

cachaça: A Brazilian rum distilled from sugarcane juice, cachaça has a sweet taste and a subtle rum flavor, with overtones of vanilla and various herbal flavors.

Calvados: A fine, powerful apple brandy made in France. Similar products include applejack from the US and apple brandy from England.

Campari: A popular Italian bitter aperitif with a brilliant red hue and strong quinine underpinnings.

Chambord: A raspberry-based liqueur made in France.

Champagne: The sparkling white wines produced from the Champagne region in France.

Chartreuse: A complex, aromatic liqueur which has been made by Carthusian monks near Grenoble, France, since 1605; it is available in both yellow and green versions.

Cherry Heering: A brand of rich, flavorsome cherry liqueur from Denmark.

chili-infused vodka: Vodka that has had chilies soaking in it until the flavor imparts the spirit; see also Flavored spirits, in Ingredients.

Cognac: A very fine brandy which is aged in special oak casks for 60 or 70 years.

crème de cacao: Chocolate-flavored liqueur, available in both white and dark.

crème de cassis: A black currant-flavored liqueur.

crème de framboise: A raspberry-flavored liqueur.

crème de mûre: A blackberry-flavored liqueur.

curaçao: An intense orange-flavored liqueur made from the peels of green oranges from the island of Curaçao. Available in clear orange and blue.

Dubonnet: A fortified wine from France.

eau-de-vie framboise sauvage: Wild raspberry brandy.

eau-de-vie de fraise: Strawberry brandy; also called framboise.
fraise des bois: A version of crème de fraise (liqueur) using wild strawberries.

glossary

framboise: see Eau-de-vie de fraise.

Frangelico: An Italian hazelnut and herb liqueur.

fruit liqueurs: Flavored liqueurs (banana, quince, raspberry, ginger, cherry, strawberry, lychee etc) which are sweet and mainly used as mixers in cocktails.

gin: A finely distilled spirit based on grains but characteristically flavored by additional blends of herbs and fruits; gin is not aged.

ginger juice: The liquid extracted from ginger when crushed or put through a juice extractor.

ginger syrup: A ginger-flavored syrup (see also Syrups, in Ingredients).

Jaggard Original: An Australian liqueur made from quandongs (a bush plum). Substitute plum juice, plum liqueur or slivovitz.

Kahlúa: A brand of sweet, rich coffee-flavored liqueur; originally from Mexico.

lemon verbena liqueur: A liqueur made from the lemon-scented leaves of lemon verbena.

Licor 43: A vanilla-flavored Spanish liqueur.

Lillet: A vermouth made with wine, fruit juice and herbs. Available white (Lillet Blanc) or red (Lillet Rouge).

lime cordial: A nonalcoholic syrup used as a mixer in drinks.

lychee juice: The juice from crushed and strained lychees.

Mandarin Napoleon: A type of curaçao, made with the skins of tangerines.

Monin Lime: A French liqueur flavored with limes.

Old Krupnik: A Polish honey liqueur.

orange bitters: A type of bitters with an orange base.

orgeat syrup: An almond-flavored syrup.

Pimms: An English liqueur flavored with fruit extracts.

pisco: A Latin American brandy.

prosecco: An Italian sparkling wine.

Poire William: A delicately flavored French pear eau-de-vie.

rum (dark, white and golden): one of the five main spirits, rum is made from sugarcane juice or molasses and comes in varying strengths and flavors. Notable brands include Bacardi, Captain Morgan, Havana Club and Mount Gay.

sake: A Japanese liquor produced from rice, commonly known as rice wine.

schnapps: Distilled, intensely flavored sweet liqueurs, schnapps is available in many varieties, from peach and apple to hazelnut or butterscotch.

Scotch whisky: Any of the whiskys made in Scotland.

slivovitz: A fruit brandy or eau-de-vie from Europe, made with black plums.

sloe gin: Gin flavored with the fruit of the wild blackthorn bush.

sour cherry syrup: A sweet, cherry-flavored nonalcoholic syrup.

tequila: A spirit distilled from the root of the blue agave plant and available in various types, including blanco (white) tequila, which is the original colorless version.

Triple Sec: An orange-flavored liqueur.

vodka: Originally distilled from potatoes but now more commonly made from grains, this highly refined spirit is colorless, odorless and flavorless; but flavored vodkas are also available (see Absolut).

index

A
Adam's apple 47
Alasia 45
Affogato 106
Apple
    Adam's apple 47
    Apple man 76
    Apple martini 53
Apricot shaker, Peach and 99
Audience martini 54

B
Banana
    Banana and pineapple refresher 67
    Banana fizz 67
    Golden banana 68
Bar spoon 11
Beetle 56
Bellini 30
Berry caipiroska 79
Berry martini 54
Berry splice 63
Berry surprise 71
Blackberry emergency 88
Blanc 100
Blending 13
Blood berries 96
Blood orange crush 77
Bloody Mary 39
Brandy Alexander 40
Building 13

C
Caiperol 80
Caipirinha 32
Caipiroska 79
Candy pop 60
Caper and chilli juice 64
Champagne flute 9
Cherry
    Cherry tree 96
    Croatian cherry 47
    Citrus fountain 92
Cocktail glass 9
Coconut holiday 72
Coffee
    Affogato 106
    Coretto 107
Collins glass 9
Coretto 107
Cosmopolitan 37
Cranberry and apple sour 91
Crenshaw 104
Croatian cherry 47
Crown martini 53

D
Daiquiri 38
Decorations 16–19

E
Eau de coing 80
Equipment 10–11

F
Flavored spirits 15
Food 20–23
French 76 44
Fruit daiquiris 71
Fruit purée 15

G
Garnishes 16–19
Gimlet 31
Gin club 81
Ginger
    Ginger and mandarin sea breeze 92
    Ginger and peach punch 105
    Ginger melon 84
    Ginger mojito 80
    Ginger 'n' orange 86
    Gingerene 91
Glasses 8–9
Golden banana 68
Grand mango 60
Grapefruit caiproska 79
Grasshopper 35
Green fairy 100
Guava vogue 93
Guide to measurements 9

H
Hazelnut martini 53
Highball glass 9
Honey martini 54
Honeydew and kiwifruit daiquiri 64

J
Jaggard crush 80
James Bond 28
Jigger 11

K
Killer martini 50
King 88
Kir royale 31
Kiwifruit daiquiri, Honeydew and 64

L
Lemon warhead 56

index

Lifesaver 88
Long Island iced tea 27
Lychee caipiroska 79

M
Mai tai 41
Mango, Grand 60
Manhattan 28
Margarita 33
Margarita no. 5 99
Martini glass 9
Measurements, Note on 9
Mint julep 36
Mixing techniques 12–13
Mojito 39
Moscow mule 29
Muddler 11
Muddling 12
Mulled wine 107

N
Napoleon 92

O
Old-fashioned glass 9
One-five-one 46

P
Passion fruit caipiroska 79

Peach
    Bellini 30
    French 75 44
    Ginger and peach
        punch 105
    Peach and apricot
        shaker 99
    Peach bubbles 44
Pear daiquiri 72
Pimms and green tea
    refresher 100
Pina colada 32
Pine lime crush 78
Pineapple
    Banana and pineapple
        refresher 67
    Pina colada 32
    Pine lime crush 78
Pisco sour 84
Plum daiquiri, Slivovitz 63

Q
Quince Eau de coing 80

R
Raspberry
    Alasia 45
    Raspberry Collins 97
    Raspberry sourgear 96

Rob Roy 40
Rocks glass 9
Rose water and cinnamon
    martini 53

S
Sake martini 56
Scoloco 99
Scud martini 50
Sea breeze 35
Sgroppino 68
Shaker 10
Shaking 13
Singapore sling 27
Slivovitz plum daiquiri 63
Soda and citrus 92
Soda nut 87
Sour morning 101
Spitfire 99
Stirring 13
Strainer 11
Strange keys 56
Strawberry
    Berry splice 63
    Strawberry Hills 98
    Strawfruit 104
    Wild strawberries 90
Sugar syrup 15
Sunshine 88

Syrups 15

T
Tangerine
    Tangerine cooler 76
    Tangerine sour 96
Tiberian sun 87
Tom Collins 36
Tomato
    Bloody Mary 39
    Caper and chilli juice 64
Tropicana 104
Tutti frutti 104

V
Vanilla martini 54
Verbs 100

W
Watermelon
    Ginger melon 84
    Watermelon martini 57
Wild strawberries 90
Wine, Mullled 107
Winter warmer 107

First published in the United States in 2003 by Periplus Editions (HK) Ltd.,
with editorial offices at 153 Milk Street, Boston, Massachusetts 02109
and 130 Joo Seng Road #06-01/03 Singapore 368357

© Copyright 2003 Lansdowne Publishing Pty Ltd

Library of Congress Cataloging-in-Publication Data is available.
ISBN 0-7946-5019-8

DISTRIBUTED BY

North America and Latin America
Tuttle Publishing
Distribution Center
Airport Industrial Park
364 Innovation Drive
North Clarendon, VT 05759-9436
Tel: (802) 773-8930
Tel: (800) 526-2778
info@tuttlepublishing.com

Japan
Tuttle Publishing
Yaekari Building, 3rd Floor
5-4-12 Ōsaki, Shinagawa-ku
Tokyo 141 0032
Tel: (03) 5437-0171
Fax: (03) 5437-0755
tuttle-sales@gol.com

Asia Pacific
Berkeley Books Pte. Ltd.
130 Joo Seng Road
#06-01/03
Singapore 368357
Tel: (65) 6280-3320
Fax: (65) 6280-6290
inquiries@periplus.com.sg

Commissioned by Deborah Nixon
Text: James Butler and Vicki Liley
Introduction text: Angus Cameron
Photographer: Steve Brown
Stylist: Vicki Liley
Designer: Grant Slaney, The Modern Art Production Group
Editor: Carolyn Miller
Production Manager: Sally Stokes
Project Coordinator: Bettina Hodgson

First Edition
06 05 04 03   10 9 8 7 6 5 4 3 2 1

All rights reserved. No part of this publication may be reproduced or utilized in
any form or by any means, electronic or mechanical, including photocopying,
recording, or by any information storage and retrieval system,
without prior written permission from the publisher.

Set in Helvetica on QuarkXPress
Printed in Singapore